Executive In Sweatpants

Executive In Sweatpants
Redefining "Business Casual"

*A Handbook for Launching
Your Work from Home Career*

by Matt Keener

Executive in Sweatpants
Copyright © 2012 Keener Marketing Solutions, LLC
www.ExecutiveInSweatpants.com

Published by:
Keener Marketing Solutions, LLC
www.KeenerMarketingSolutions.com

Dedicated to my mom and dad
who have always inspired me to
pursue excellence in everything I do.

I would also like to thank my friends
Jeff Meltzer, Alan Wooldridge, Dr. Michael Carr, and Steve Holt
who have helped me in many ways.

Table of Contents

Chapter 1 Executive In Sweatpants 1

Chapter 2 The $9 Ironing Board 7

Chapter 3 Salary Is A Dead-End Proposition. 17

Chapter 4 Don't Quit Your Day Job...Yet. 25

Chapter 5 Tear Up the Fancy Parchment Paper 35

Chapter 6 The New "Digital You" 41

Chapter 7 Let's Make a Deal 51

Chapter 8 Building Your Client Base. 63

Chapter 9 Tracking Your Success. 71

Chapter 10 Setting Boundaries 79

Chapter 11 You Must Keep Learning. 85

Chapter 12 Let's Go Shopping for Sweatpants! 95

Bonus Chapter: Secret Free Tools 99

Chapter 1:
Executive In Sweatpants

Yep. You guessed it. I'm wearing sweatpants right now. Although it may seem like an absurd concept, I view my sweatpants as a distinct privilege - a status symbol for the Twenty First Century. Who needs Dockers when you can wear Reebok all day...

But, as you may have guessed, I have not always been an "Executive in Sweatpants". On the contrary, at one time I was much like you - working lots of hours for a fixed salary, trying to climb the corporate ladder, etc. The worst part was that I had to wear slacks every day. (I hate ironing!)

Our nation's culture tells us that in order to be deemed "successful", it is important to operate within certain norms. A large home, a reputable job with a big company, a new car, and an expensive wardrobe are all symbols that indicate one's success.

In this book, I intend to turn all of these assumptions upside down and provide you with an action-oriented plan for true success in today's economy. The only prerequisite for becoming an Executive in Sweatpants is that you keep a very open mind. Check all of your preconceived notions at the door.

So Why Sweatpants?

Perhaps the question should be "why not sweatpants?". I like to watch football games in sweatpants. I like to read books in sweatpants. I even sleep in sweatpants in the winter. So why wouldn't I wear sweatpants to work?

You may be thinking to yourself, "Yes, I'd love to work in sweatpants.... But my company has strict policies relating to dress codes." Quite simply, this mentality is exactly the problem. You have placed limitations on your potential by thinking only within the confines of your current employer's HR handbook. Corporations have rules like these in place for good reason. Hundreds of locations and thousands of employees need to have some cohesive structure to ensure organizational goals are being met. But what about your goals? What about your dreams?

As humans, we get into routines. We like a sense of normalcy. Many of us spend so much time and energy avoiding life's "uncomfortable" moments that we lose our willingness to take calculated risks. I contend that we are only able to achieve our true potential by stepping out of our comfort zone.

Some of the greatest achievements in my career have developed because I was able to overcome my own anxieties. I'm inherently a modest, mild-mannered Midwesterner. Early in my career, I would get extremely nervous in new business situations. Meeting new people, making a good first impression, and speaking off the cuff really made me quiver. This became especially obvious when I took on my first sales position.

In some of my initial experiences with clients and vendors from New York City, I quickly learned that I needed to step up my game. After dealing with certain customers, I felt like I had just gone a few rounds with Mike Tyson. However, over time I really grew to respect people who can make it in the Big Apple. In a city with 8 million citizens, you have to be tough to thrive.

In my observations, I have noticed that successful New Yorkers all have something in common: lack of fear. Whether negotiating a better price, pitching new business ideas, or jumping into a burning building after 9/11, New Yorkers stand out in my mind as the essence of fortitude overcoming fear. This lesson is one of the most important I've learned. Being able to overcome your anxieties is a continual process, but it is crucial in your journey to become an Executive in Sweatpants.

It Comes Down To Perspective

Unless you knew better, you may reasonably assume that someone who works in sweats all day would have a lackadaisical work ethic. I have to admit, this would have probably been my reaction just a few years ago. Whether we admit it or not, we are all trained to view situations through the norms of our society. But things aren't always how they seem; on the contrary, things are often the opposite of how they seem. Our perspective plays a major role in the decisions we make and the level of success we achieve.

For example, consider a worker at your local Starbucks (since I like their coffee). When I visit Starbucks, the lady behind the counter enters my order, takes payment, makes my drink to my exact specification, alerts me when my drink is ready, and courteously says, "Have a great day" as I leave. For all of these services, she has agreed to work for a menial, flat hourly wage with little hope of meaningful fulfillment from her job. To top it off, she has to comply with Starbucks' dress code! Although I give her credit for working hard and providing a good service, I would challenge the line of thinking that lead her to that position.

My point here is that most Americans only think "within the box" of what society leads them to believe. "There aren't any jobs in my town.".... "This recession is making it hard to find a good job.".... "I wish my boss wasn't such a jerk." These thoughts often make us "settle" for something as opposed to living our dreams.

Why only look for opportunities within the confines of your city? Why do you choose to participate in the recession? Why do you put all of your faith in a single employer? Why bother even having a boss?

You will notice that a key theme throughout this book will be the importance of your perspective. "Going with the flow" usually leads you exactly where everyone else is - broke and hopeless.

My Sweatpants Are A Metaphor. Kind Of…

By now you might be wondering why I chose to focus so much on sweatpants and if I'm really going to keep this theme throughout the book's entirety. Let's be clear - I don't really care what you wear.

The point is that I have the absolute freedom to wear sweatpants each day. If you're reading this book, chances are you don't have this freedom yet. I have the absolute freedom to start my workday at 5 am, 7:15 am, or 9:08 am. You don't. I have the absolute freedom to never be stuck in a traffic jam, driving to an office that I don't like. You don't. I have the absolute freedom to set my own schedule, pick who my customers will be, and negotiate how much I will be paid. You don't.

Doesn't it make you mad that you are missing out on these freedoms? I'm mad on your behalf. Your employer has agreed to pay you a fixed amount of money per year in exchange for your exclusive attention. I'm not mad at your employer - your employer is just a better negotiator than you currently are. My goal is to help you realize your full potential and, in turn, take back the power you deserve.

Chapter 2:
The $9 Ironing Board

I'm always amazed how people complain when large companies close up shop and move production offshore. People who live in smaller Midwestern cities like mine are especially notorious for doing this. I've heard these people say things like, "those greedy corporations are only concerned about their profits" and "corporations put their bottom line above people".

While there may be some truth to these types of comments, there is a bigger issue we need to discuss: the $9 ironing board.

After I graduated from college, I landed a good job with a major company in my hometown. I was fortunate enough to live at home with my parents for the first few years of my career. This allowed me to save up a deposit for a nice house.

When I moved into my new home, I quickly realized there were many necessities that I needed to buy. Many of the things I took for granted while living at home were now totally my responsibility. In order to iron my slacks, do the dishes, or clean the bathrooms, I needed to stock up on supplies.

I clearly remember my first trip to Wal-Mart as a new homeowner. In college, I had gone to Wal-Mart to buy things. But this trip was different. For some reason, this was the first time it felt like I was spending "my own money". Perhaps my sizable new mortgage payment played a factor in making me feel this way.

As I scanned the Wal-Mart list I had prepared, I began to realize this was going to be an expensive trip. Bed sheets, cleaning supplies, pots and pans, silverware, light bulbs, lawn chairs, and an ironing board were just a few of the items I needed.

For some reason, I decided to start at the bottom of the list and find an ironing board. I quickly located the ironing board section and hoped that I could find one for under $25. I really had no idea how expensive an ironing board should be, but I figured this would be a fair budget amount for something so large and somewhat mechanical in nature.

To my total disbelief, I spotted a generic brand ironing board for only $9! I stood there for several moments trying to consider if a $9 ironing board would even be worth purchasing. There were several other boards I could choose from, ranging in price up to $50. I came to the conclusion that I would take my chances with the 'el-cheapo' model and just replace it if it ever broke.

Several years later, I am happy to report that the $9 ironing board is working better than ever.

Have you ever bought a $9 ironing board? If not, I bet you have at least purchased a generic product that was cheaper than the name brand version. If so, from this point forward you are never allowed to complain about companies laying off workers, moving production off shore, or some combination of both. In the long run, you can't have thousands of highly paid U.S. based manufacturing jobs and $9 ironing boards. The last time I checked, people aren't rushing out in mass to overpay for a commodity like an ironing board. Unfortunately for the American laborer, employment will have to be sought elsewhere.

Am I anti-worker? No. Am I advocating all companies close up shop and exploit cheap labor in other countries? Absolutely not. I'm simply pointing out the obvious realities of supply and demand. Consumers demand $9 ironing boards; companies are in business to increase shareholder value by generating profits; therefore, to be competitive in today's marketplace, you must know how to thrive given these axioms.

The Realities of the American Labor Market

Picture this - you are the VP of Operations for ABC Ironing Boards Inc. A recent report from the Sales & Marketing department indicates that you are rapidly losing market share to another competitor. Your 'entry level' ironing board accounts for over 50% of your sales revenue and a large percentage of corporate margins. A major strength of this product line is its outstanding distribution. The product is carried by major retailers, including Wal-Mart, Target, Costco, and Sam's Club. These four retailers comprise virtually 100% of this product line's sales.

As you read the report, you quickly realize that at this pace your market share will be whittled down to nothing. As VP of Operations, you are faced with three simple, yet daunting options.

Option 1: Match your competitor's price without changing any of the manufacturing inputs. After reviewing this scenario with the Pricing and Sales & Marketing departments, it is determined this option is not viable. Margins would be virtually nonexistent, so this option is quickly tabled.

Option 2: Match you competitor's price, but reduce manufacturing inputs in an effort to stabilize margins. With years of experience in manufacturing, you know that your company has already negotiated the lowest raw material costs possible. Your facility is already heavily automated. With the recent cash flow issues resulting from shrinking market share, additional capital investment is unlikely. You are left with only one possibility for this option - move a portion (or all) of your production to a lower cost country. Mexico, Bangladesh, and the Philippines are all viable locations you have considered in the past.

Option 3: Concede the market share to your competitor and focus on other product lines. The problem with this option is that your organization has invested significant resources to obtain the competitive position and distribution it has. Given that this product line represents over half of your company's total sales, it is urgent that you avoid this option.

So which option did you choose? If you want to keep your job and save your company from financial ruin, you likely decide to set up operations in a different country. The unfortunate reality is that hundreds of your factory workers will lose their jobs in the process.

An increasing number of companies are faced with this issue. In order to stay alive as a company and keep shareholders happy, organizations have to make these kinds of tough decisions. It is not because they want to close down their factories and put people out of jobs. On the contrary, in a perfect world, it would be much easier to keep everything domestic. Cultural, logistical, and time zone issues could be averted - not to mention all the bad press the company is likely going to get for moving offshore.

So what are all of the variables that make American labor increasingly uncompetitive in a global marketplace?

High Cost of Living In the USA - According to a recent study by the Bureau of Labor Statistics[1], the average American couple in their late twenties makes an income of $38,182 per year and has expenditures of $26,649. The average household in India makes less than $1,000

---

[1] Bureau of Labor Statistics, http://www.bls.gov/cex/anthology11/csxanth6.pdf

per year[2]. Unfortunately for Americans, we live in a global economy now - this is a hard reality that many people are now beginning to feel.

Restrictive Government Regulations - Politicians at the local, state, and federal levels continue to enact policies that kill entrepreneurship and innovation. More regulation leads to uncertainty in the marketplace and a decreased willingness by business owners to invest in human capital. I would argue that for each new law that is passed thousands of jobs are outsourced or eliminated entirely. In addition, our departure from sound money has put the final nail in the coffin of the American labor force, especially in manufacturing sectors.

Under-Motivated Populous - I believe that American ingenuity is still alive and well. However, a divide is growing between employees and the revenue stream. Society teaches us that working for a mega corporation is the most preferable route. Whether working on the production floor or in a cubicle, many fall into this trap.

However, it is difficult to stay motivated when you are far removed from the company's bottom line. As a corporation grows, the primary mission often becomes to mitigate risk (rather than push for continuous innovation). This stagnation trickles down to all levels of the company, further magnifying the motivational issues I've mentioned.

Rising Insurance & Benefit Costs - It wasn't until the 1940s that US companies began offering employee benefit plans as a way to attract better workers. The reason why employers began offering such health insurance packages was in response to government-mandated wage freezes during World War II. Over time, this became a societal norm that all companies were expected to provide. As we all know, insurance premiums and medical services have skyrocketed over the recent

[2] Stanford University, http://cee45q.stanford.edu/2003/briefing_book/india.html

decades. Business owners are left to foot the bill for such expenses.

Emerging Foreign Economies - There are several billion other people on this planet with similar desires to yours. Technology now affords many in traditionally impoverished societies to compete on a whole new level. India comes to mind once again - a large populous with a growing base of educated professionals. The country is home to an ever-expanding supply of experts in technology, general law, business systems, and more.

A Population Deeply In Debt & Living Outside of Its Means - It pains me to hear stories about young adults who come out of college with debt. Many believe going eye deep into debt is the only way to get a "good education". I fondly recall my high school graduation party - friends' parents bragging about how Johnny was going to Northwestern University[3] ($41,592 in 2012 for tuition only) to pursue a "pre-med" degree. I remember at the time thinking about how insane that decision was. Looking back, I feel deep sadness for Johnny. Regardless of his success later in life, a four year degree from Northwestern (or any comparable expensive University) started Johnny $160K in the hole. Compare that to my $0 expense for college by attending a local state university, living at home, and working hard to get tuition paid via scholarships.

Complacency Compounds the Problem

To a certain extent, American families have become increasingly complacent in the decisions they make and the perspectives they maintain. I attribute this complacency to several things.

First, our children are not really learning history. It may still be written in textbooks and taught in class, but something seems to get lost in translation. The fact that only 70 years ago, our country

---

3 Northwestern University, http://www.northwestern.edu/newscenter/stories/2011/03/costs-set.html

was engaged in a World War to defeat a regime that killed millions still boggles my mind. Things move so fast these days that it is hard imagine this happened so recently. Advancements in technology and communications make relatively recent events (such as the defeat of Nazism, Communism, and Fascism) seem like ancient history. I'm not saying that our rapid advancements in technology and communication are bad; on the contrary, the Internet is truly our last refuge for free speech. What I am saying is that our culture is moving so quickly that we fail to impart the true lessons learned from our recent past. We have become too comfortable, which has allowed other nations to pass us by in many aspects.

It is also apparent that only a small percentage of the US populous has a clue about basic free market economic theory. It is truly scary that over 20% of the US population depends on the federal government for their daily housing, food, and health care (according to the Heritage Foundation's 2010 Index of Dependence on Government[4]). The same study from Heritage found that the percentage of Americans who do not pay federal income taxes and who are not claimed as dependents by someone else has risen to 43.6%.

These stats illustrate a lack of concern for economics at all levels of society (politicians especially). If our society understood such basic principles, it would be a national priority to reduce such figures as close to zero as possible.

Surviving the $9 Ironing Board Effect

It is clear we have become a society that values the acquisition of low-cost goods (and services to some extent) more than it values domestic labor. I firmly believe that the stagnant unemployment rate (now consistently hovering well over 8%) is impacted by this phenomenon. Manufacturing in the US has largely dried up, leaving

4 Heritage Foundation, http://www.heritage.org/research/reports/2010/10/the-2010-index-of-dependence-on-government

many laborers and even white-collar workers looking for employment. High unemployment rates cause families to cut expenses even further, thus compounding the issue.

The good news is that organizations are still willing to invest money in human capital if it will provide a tangible return on investment. The concept of value is key to understand here. Stop and consider this for the moment - in your current job, have you ever tried to quantify the value that you bring to your company? Everyone loves the job that pays $100,000 plus benefits, but are you adding significantly more value than your company compensates you? Are you even close? Before reading any further, you must stop and absorb this concept. Surviving the "$9 ironing board effect" is dependent upon you being able to understand this simple, yet powerful value proposition.

Chapter 3:
Salary Is A Dead-End Proposition

All through the years of my formal education, there seemed to be a common axiom asserted by those instructing me: go to college, get a degree, and some big company will hire you. Although this path certainly has merit, it is stunning to me that the topic of value was never discussed in much detail. As we discussed in the previous chapter, understanding value is absolutely vital for thriving as an employee or vendor. Likewise, it is equally important for employers to consider when making hiring decisions. This chapter will help you understand the psychology of how an employer looks at staffing and what it means for your long-term personal success.

As I mentioned, when I graduated from college I went to work for a major corporation in my hometown. [I had the good fortune of doing an internship before graduation, which lead to a full time position with the company. Internships are one of the great things about working for a big company. Not only can you learn from hands-on experiences, you can also make the right connections to start your climb up the corporate ladder (if that is your goal).] When I hired on full time my official title was "Marketing Analyst". This position was not too focused on one particular responsibility; rather, it allowed me to get a broad perspective of the corporate world. I was able to get a flavor for project management, brand management, commercialization, pricing strategy, and occasionally some corporate backslapping.

My starting salary was $45,000 plus benefits and a 401K match (up to a certain percentage). Not too shabby for a guy fresh out of college in a smaller Midwest city. In all honesty, I kind of expected to be offered this type of package when I graduated. In my naive mind, I deserved it. I had gotten the degree, received the academic accolades, and was ready to cash in professionally.

Your Personal Profit & Loss Statement

I specifically remember the feeling of excitement when I saw my nameplate attached to my office door (let's be honest, it was a cubicle with no door). It was a feeling that I had "arrived" and all the hard work in college was paying off. The corporate world is funny like that; little things such as nameplates, office size, and job titles help formulate your perceived level of power within the organization. In fact, many management books I have read discuss this very topic. Large organizations leverage different power structures (such as legitimate power, coercive power, etc.) to develop their cultures.

Big companies leverage such strategies for many reasons; however, I believe a major cause for such structure is due to simple economics. A company can only afford to pay an employee less than what value they contribute. I like to think of this as a "personal profit & loss statement". Are you adding more value (i.e. profit) than what you are being paid (i.e. the company's loss). Much like a P&L statement for the entire company, your "personal P&L" considers how much you increase the company's reserves in relation to how much you withdraw.

There are many ways you can impact your personal P&L within an organization: increasing sales, decreasing costs, enhancing the company's brand or image, improving the efficiency of business processes, etc. Basically, doing any type of activity that enhances the company's net income will make your value within the company more obvious.

By nature, some activities are more closely correlated with the performance of the company. Take for example a sales representative.

This is the easiest personal P&L to calculate. In most sales departments, if you don't sell anything you don't get paid much (if anything). The idea of "pay for performance" has traditionally been a staple of sales positions. Compensation is typically pegged as a percentage of total sales receipts. As such, the company can closely control its maximum out of pocket expense of employing a sales representative (at least percentage-wise), without limiting the earning potential of the sales rep. These types of relationships are truly a win-win; however, they require a special skill set. Not many people are comfortable with the idea of working in sales.

Now, let's take a somewhat inverse role (and something dear to my heart): marketing. In theory, the efforts of a marketing department should be somewhat measurable. As I will explain later on, marketing efforts are indeed quite measurable within smaller organizations. However, in a large company, marketing can easily be viewed as a supporting function and not one that impacts bottom line performance. I attribute this to two main reasons. First, the marketing departments of larger firms (and often other non-sales functions, such as legal and HR) focus primarily on averting risk. It is almost impossible to quantify how much risk is being averted at a given point in time. Perhaps even more impossible to quantify is how such aversion will impact the organization's profit and loss. Second, with regard specifically to marketing, large corporations often spend their time on brand-building activities (marketing literature development, communications management, and commercialization management, etc.). Like risk aversion, brand management is also difficult to quantify in terms of value.

As you may have guessed, the reason I present such examples is to make you consider the value you are adding to an organization. Whether you work for someone else or you own your own business, the value you provide is how you will be judged. This impacts your compensation, job security, and other factors that people like to discuss.

Outpacing Your "Cost" Without Limiting Your Earning Potential

You might have noticed the title of this chapter is "Salary Is A Dead-End Proposition". So far, we've only discussed your perceived value. It's now time to look at the other side of the coin: are you providing **too much value** for your compensation? In other words, are you under-compensated?

The natural reaction from many people to this question would be a resounding "yes". Most people feel that their salaries should be increased based on their own perception of value. This, of course, tends to be a biased evaluation of one's own situation. However, your monetary value is truly a function of two determinants: options and scarcity.

Let's first look at options. If you provide outstanding services but have no other options for employment, your earning potential is thus minimized. An employer is much more likely to pay you a higher wage if he feels like others might steal you away. If other companies understand the value you could provide them, the earning potential with your current employer increases.

In a similar way, employers consider scarcity when determining the wages they pay. Obviously there are more people in the world who can stuff envelopes than can run advanced pricing models. As such, scarcity of the skill set significantly impacts one's earning potential.

As a side note, I believe the "corporatization" of Western societies has changed the very basics of how we look at employment. Although corporations have done (and continue to do) infinite levels of good for living standards, corporatization has also negatively impacted the way our society views employment. By narrowly defining the roles of each employee within an organization, corporations have developed tremendous efficiencies. Employees who are cast into narrowly defined roles are often unable to realize their fullest potential. Although it may be beneficial to have someone in charge of toilet paper acquisition, that role is very far from the sales pipeline and the true mission of the company. As such, many employees become easily disgruntled and lose interest in their work. After all, there is only so much savings one can reap from pitting toilet paper vendors against one another in a bidding war.

If you have multiple options for employment and some level of scarcity in your skill set, your market value will demand a premium. The million-dollar question is how to best accomplish this goal. For many Americans, the idea of exploring additional income streams (beyond a current employer) only becomes a reality when it is too late. Market fluctuations cause a need for corporate downsizing, thus eliminating otherwise stable employment. Developing a winning strategy for avoiding these trends is key to your success.

Making The Case for Multiple Employers

At this point in the book, I want to start making the case for the business model I have developed: working for multiple clients from the comfort of home. We will get into the details of how to actually do this later in the book. In this section we will look at the mathematics and risk factors you should consider.

For discussion, let's imagine a young marketing professional named Brad Michaels is at a crossroads in his life. He's worked for a mid-sized corporation (American Widget Corporation) for the past decade. He has some interest in climbing the corporate ladder but has no desire to relocate. Deep down, Brad has always thought of himself as an entrepreneur but was never really willing or able to take the full plunge. A couple years ago, a former classmate made Brad aware of freelance networking websites such as www.oDesk.com and www. Elance.com (more information to come later about these great tools). Brad created an oDesk account and was able to get some occasional freelance marketing work. Recently, several of his clients on oDesk have inquired about Brad's availability for additional hours. Brad is now at a decision point: should he choose the corporate ladder or take a chance on his dream of self-employment? Let's look at the trade offs.

Option 1: Stay Focused on the Corporate Ladder

If Brad stays put, there is a good likelihood that he will continue to progress in the organization's management hierarchy. His salary will increase annually by 3% for the rest of his career, until he is able to achieve an executive management position (such as Chief Marketing Officer or SVP Sales & Marketing).

Option 2: Take A Chance on the American Dream of Entrepreneurism

If Brad resigns from American Widget Corp and focuses exclusively on building his own consulting business, he would experience an immediate pay cut of about 50%. Although his hourly rate would be higher than what American Widget is paying, he would only have 20 hours filled per week (given his current clients' work requirements). He currently has four clients and would need four more to get 40 billable hours per week (and equal his current salary at American Widget).

At first glance, option 1 seems like the safest decision for Brad. However, I would argue that Brad needs to think seriously about his risk factor by staying with American Widget. In today's world of rapidly evolving markets and stagnant economies, very few companies are immune from sales fluctuations and downsizing. Brad could be the best worker in the company, but if the organization decides to outsource its marketing or goes out of business, Brad is out of luck. By choosing to take the "safe" option in the short term, Brad could actually be choosing the more risky proposition in the long run.

Now I realize very few people look at employment in the way I've just described. But just consider this: if Brad could earn the exact same amount of money by working from home, why wouldn't he? Besides, he would be significantly reducing his risk factor by having 8 different income streams (versus a single income stream at American Widget). So what is stopping him from pursuing his dream? Other than a little hard work, not much is stopping him.

Chapter 4:
Don't Quit Your Day Job…Yet

In the previous chapter we talked about Brad Michaels. In either situation, Brad could make a viable argument that he is pursuing the correct path. Although I would encourage Brad to take the leap into the entrepreneurial world, he could easily rationalize staying put at American Widget. Brad could justify either option because he has viable options to choose from. If he stays, he has a seemingly secure job. If he leaves, he has a solid base of existing clients to build from.

So what about you? You might be thinking about quitting your corporate job and starting a business. There are countless companies that claim to help you start a work from home business for only a "nominal fee". Before you sign up for any seminars or commit to one of these programs (which are mostly scams), I suggest you start by examining your skills that could be marketable. Perhaps you are a good writer, know about social networking, have a strategic planning background, or a background in finance. Regardless your skill set, start by thinking about what you're good at and what you enjoy doing.

Learning the Hard Way - My Story

My journey to becoming an Executive in Sweatpants was a bit bumpier than our friend Brad Michaels. As I mentioned, after graduating from college I started working for a big corporation as a Marketing Analyst. I really enjoyed this job, but I've always had an entrepreneurial streak. Although I liked the security and structure of a 9 to 5 corporate job, self-employment was always in the back of my mind. I'm one of those guys who is always coming up with ideas for inventions and new products.

A few years into my career, the company I was working for decided to launch a new division focused on developing non-core technologies and business units. Given that the company specialized in somewhat boring things (at least to me) such as automotive components, the opportunity to expand into more interesting product lines was attractive. The company's logic for starting this new division was to reduce the dependency on new vehicle builds (which are quite cyclical in nature) by pursuing adjacent markets and incubating new product lines.

I decided to apply for a position within the new department. After an interview with the department head, they offered me the job. I let my existing boss know and started preparing for my new role. It all happened quickly, but every step of the process seemed like it was meant to be. Looking back, I think my entrepreneurial spirit had taken the reigns, and I was just along for the ride.

At first, our corporate management was on board with the department's mission: identify new technologies we could commercialize within existing or adjacent markets. However, as time went on and management roles changed, support for our department became less obvious.

I had been assigned a project that involved a variety of technologies. My job was to work with the inventors, understand the full potential of the market, and help commercialize the products. After a few months of work, it became clear that only one of the technologies was ready to be marketed. The unfortunate thing (at least for me) was that this particular product line was the most unusual among the technologies allocated to my project. This product line involved some unique 3D (three dimensional) optical technologies and printing capabilities. Originally, this 3D technology was viewed somewhat as an add-on to sweeten the deal for the most applicable technology (which involved some unique reflective materials and had direct application in the transportation industry).

Although it seemed like a stretch at the time, I was determined to make the best of the situation and help my company succeed in this new endeavor. As you might imagine, this new division (and perhaps more specifically the 3D project) created some friction internally.

I clearly remember my first run-in with the IT department. I had just returned from being away on my honeymoon. Apparently, while I was gone, a bunch of 3D equipment had been delivered to the office, raising eyebrows about what had been ordered. As I approached my cubicle, I noticed there was a crowd of IT guys congregating around the cubicle next to mine. The IT department head said to me in a somewhat sarcastic tone, "What have you been ordering, Matt?". I gave a puzzled look back to him and noticed that some of the guys in the group were snickering almost with glee. I walked toward the adjacent cubicle and peeked inside. The cubicle was packed full of digital equipment, supplies, and other materials. Each package had my name prominently displayed on the label for all to see. I felt a sinking feeling in my stomach, as I realized that some were not happy with this new endeavor and probably thought that I was an idiot. The IT manager made it clear that anything plugged into any wall had to be approved by him. It would have been nice to know that little tidbit before all the materials were ordered and shipped to the company at my attention.

My IT department run-in demonstrates the growing pains of incubating a small business within a large corporation. Although everyone likes the general idea of incubating new revenue streams and product lines, things can quickly change. Having been involved with several small business launches, I can tell you that it is stressful enough to launch a new business when you are only accountable to yourself (i.e. the owner). It is even more difficult to do this within a corporation, as you have the added worries of what your colleagues think about you. Trying to launch a 3D graphics business within an automotive company is an extreme example. However, my point is that starting a business within a corporation is quite difficult, regardless the nature of the product.

As time went on, we began to make some traction with the 3D product line. We had several large customers interested in the technology and felt that sizable orders could be on the horizon. However, market conditions changed, and our time was growing short. My boss got the vibe that the project (and perhaps the entire department) would be cancelled by the company. Both my boss and I still saw the potential of the 3D product line and felt that the other technologies (namely the reflective material) could be equally successful in the future. After lengthy discussions, we decided it would be worthwhile to continue developing these technologies as an independent company regardless of the nature of the product.

My boss was able to negotiate a deal that would allow him to leave the company and acquire the rights to the technology. He made me an offer to come onboard as a minority owner in the business. I viewed this as a huge opportunity for my professional career. I realized there would be no guarantee of income other than what I was able to successfully acquire in new business. I liked the idea of being part of something fresh and growing a brand from the ground up. Looking back, I still can't believe that I left my cushy job for such uncertainty. However, at the time, there was no question in my mind that it was the right decision.

So You're An Entrepreneur... Now What?

Before I knew it, I was waking up at 5:15 am and working until about 6 pm each day. Lounging around on Saturday was a thing of the past too. I quickly went from working 40 hours per week to well over 60. Some weeks I would work over 70 hours. When your only hope for a paycheck depends upon your ability to make profitable sales, the phrase "hard work" takes on a whole new meaning.

Given the nature of the product line, our main strategy was to chase large potential contracts. Our business model was based on doing custom design work in-house and then outsourcing the manufacturing once we procured the contract. As you might imagine, the problem with this business model is that it yields significant peaks and valleys in cash flow (and thus personal income). In fact, it was about six months of deep valleys until we got our first big sale. It had been such a long, arduous six months that I really could not believe it when we received the purchase order from the client.

Still being somewhat naive, I assumed that this sizable order would solve all of our problems. On the contrary, I quickly found out how a large order can nearly destroy a small company. Keep in mind, we had virtually zero cash inflow from clients leading up to this big order. However, we had incurred all kinds of expenses during the six months. Rent, design fees, supplies, and travel expenses had all been accruing each month. As I began to examine the cost of goods sold from our "big" order, I quickly realized that the "profit" would barely cover the overhead expenses we had incurred leading up to that point. What a deflating feeling!

Perhaps the worst part about the order was the terms of sale. As I mentioned, this order was a sizable order for our company. Sizable orders typically come from companies that have sizable bank accounts.

However, sizable companies also have significant negotiating power. Such companies use their negotiating power to yield maximum cash flow benefits to themselves, thus making a company like ours act essentially like a bank. I'm not complaining about this fact; it just is what it is. After we received the purchase order, thankfully we were able to get a small deposit. We used this money to make a deposit to our supplier, thus yielding a neutral cash flow event for our company. The order was slated to take around 30 days to fulfill. During this time, there would be zero additional payments from our customer. After our customer received the order, they had net 30 days to pay us the balance due. If you add up the days, it means we would not get a penny of profit until 60 days after we received the purchase order (assuming everything went to plan). During this two-month period, we still had more overhead costs that had to be paid. By the time we received final payment, overhead expenses had eaten up any potential profit.

Reality Sets In

The cash flow situation I've described is typical of many startup companies. At the time, I kept telling myself that eventually we would get enough "big orders" to justify our existence and make a profit. The lure of large potential orders in the pipeline was certainly tempting. But after about a year of peaks and valleys, I had to do something else to stabilize my family's cash flow. I wasn't ready to give up on the technology we were marketing; however, I had to find a way to make more money for my family. Thankfully, my wife had a good job as a teacher. This allowed us to take the entrepreneurial risk in the first place. But in the long run, living off my wife's salary was not my vision of success.

I decided that it was my responsibility to find a part-time job that would yield my family some additional income. Even if it were only a few hundred extra dollars per month, it would be a big boost to my confidence. After months of feeling like a failure, any level of success can go a long way.

The first idea I had was to get a paper route. As silly as this seemed, I figured I could deliver papers early in the morning and then go into the office after finishing my route. This idea lost steam when I realized that our local newspaper was not hiring. My next idea was even worse. Since I had a background in marketing, I knew there were websites that would pay you to take online surveys. I signed up for several accounts and got to work. However, I quickly realized that although the surveys did pay you for your opinion, it was rarely worth the effort. I began to time my efforts and realized my effective hourly rate was way less than minimum wage. Strike two.

Then, I stumbled upon oDesk.com… and my whole world changed forever.

PART II:
THE NEW PARADIGM OF BUSINESS

Chapter 5:
Tear Up the Fancy Parchment Paper

I had heard radio commercials advertising this idea of "work from home", but I never really thought it could be for real. I mean, I did know that some bigger companies were starting to allow their employees to "tele-commute" occasionally, but that was different. Outside of this exception, I had already formed a stereotype that "work from home" careers basically meant you were unemployed and played around on the Internet somehow.

When I came across oDesk.com, something clicked inside my brain. For those of you who have never heard of oDesk, allow me to introduce you. Here is the company's summary blurb directly from their website[5]:

> oDesk offers the world's largest, most comprehensive and fastest-growing online workplace.
>
> Businesses are no longer limited to local talent or traditional hiring cycles. With a thriving online workforce available on-demand, you can post a job for free, field applications in hours and rapidly hire the best person for the job, regardless of where in the world they happen to be.
>
> If you are looking for work, you are now untethered by geography. Find work and get the job done from anywhere. All you need is your talent, a computer and an Internet connection.
>
> oDesk doesn't just connect businesses and independent professionals. Our patent-pending technology gives you a virtual workspace, offering real-time visibility into work as it happens. Payment is quick and hassle-free.

5 oDesk, https://www.odesk.com/info/about/

More online work happens on oDesk than anywhere else on the web. In 2011 alone, businesses posted over a million jobs and contractors earned more than $220 million.

Let me translate: oDesk is an online recruiting tool, hiring platform, automated timecard, performance review system, and payroll processor built into a single global marketplace of clients and freelance contractors. Thousands of companies (both small and large) are online right now actively recruiting for virtually every kind of role. If it can be done on a computer, it can be done using work from home talent.

A Comparison To Another Familiar Marketplace

I like to compare oDesk to an eBay for professional services. Think about how you have used eBay in the past. Let's imagine that you have a hard time finding your favorite brand of jeans in local department stores. You've looked all over the city, but no one seems to keep them in stock. So, in an effort to find them, you get on eBay. You type in the name brand, size, and color and instantly several appear in the search results. You place a bid on the pants, win the auction, pay for the jeans, and a few days later the pants arrive in your mailbox. In this example, eBay acted as the middleman between you (i.e. the person in demand of a certain product) and the merchant (i.e. the person supplying the product). You are happy because you found the jeans that are impossible to find in your town. The merchant is happy because he sold his product for a profit. eBay is happy because they took a percentage of the transaction.

oDesk acts much like eBay, but obviously in a different capacity. Instead of facilitating the sale of physical goods, oDesk facilitates the exchange of professional business services. So let's image that you own an ice cream shop in New York City. When looking at your profit and loss statement for the previous year, you realize that your net income was about 10% lower than what you were expecting. You suspect that your overhead is killing your profitability, but you aren't for sure. What are your options for trying to figure out the issue? First, you could try to look at the data yourself and try to diagnose the issue. However, you're not really trained in cost accounting - you're more of a sales and marketing guy. Instead, you could call up your accountant down on 42nd street, but you quickly realize that he charges $150 per hour. Diagnosing the issue might cost more than the issue itself! So what do you do now? Enter oDesk into the equation.

How oDesk Works - From 30,000 Feet

Without getting into the technical details of how oDesk works (that comes later), the process of finding an affordable expert to assist you is really quite easy. In a nutshell, it looks something like this:

1. **Create a free account on oDesk.**

2 **Post the job to the oDesk marketplace.** (either as a "public" job or "private" job)

   a. If you post the job as "public", you will get hundreds of applicants from all over the world. The hourly rate of the applicants who apply will likely be between $5 and $100 per hour, with the majority being people off shore and less than $10 per hour.

   b If you post the job as "private", only those who you invite will be able to see the job. In order to identify candidates, oDesk gives you all kinds of filters to weed through possible contractors. Filters for the contractor's location, feedback score, hourly rate, and other details are available to let you find exactly the talent you are looking for. Once you have identified a few candidates that meet your needs, you can send them an invitation to interview.

3. Interview the candidates (obviously the interview would not be in person, but rather over the phone).

4. Hire the contractor. Note: The contractor will run oDesk's software while working on your project. oDesk automatically tracks the contractor's hours and pays the contractor based on the parameters you set in the contract.

5. Leave feedback after the project is complete

Now as you can imagine, there are many details to how this process actually works. I will go into great detail later in the book about pitfalls to avoid (for both contractors and hiring firms). But in the simple process I've outlined above, you can begin to see the power of using a tool like oDesk. Below are a few of the more obvious benefits:

- Instant access to millions of talented professionals that fit your exact budget.

- Total transparency into your project - oDesk takes automatic screenshots of your contractor's computer while he or she is working, giving you the ability to review the quality of work before receiving the final deliverable.

- Zero payroll headaches - oDesk will automatically create and distribute 1099s for each individual contractor.

- Zero payroll tax - They're not your employees - no payroll taxes required.

- Less risk than dealing with a traditional contractor - Leverage the power of oDesk's feedback system to ensure you get the results you want from your contractor.

So Why Should I Care?

Last time I checked, the unemployment rate in the United States is hovering somewhere between 8% and 10% (based on how the data is being manipulated). When you factor in people who are considered "underemployed" or those who have given up looking for work, we have a sizable population that should care.

Let's go back to the original title of this chapter ("Tear Up the Fancy Parchment Paper"). What exactly am I referring to in this title? It is really quite simple - a major reason why so many are struggling to find employment is because they are using tactics from the 1990s and early 2000s. In the "old days", companies would post jobs in newspapers or on websites such as www.Monster.com and wait to see how many people apply. During times of low unemployment, such postings may only yield a few hundred applicants. Therefore, it was much easier for applicants to get attention. You might have been able to submit your resume and receive a call from the HR department within a few days. Today, millions of people are competing for only a handful of full-time positions. Instead of a simple job posting yielding a few hundred applicants, it is now yielding many thousand qualified applicants. How do you like your odds?

It is human nature to fight change. The problem is that sending paper resumes or submitting online applications is not working for many in our society. So why do Americans spend so much time massaging their resumes? Why are there "resume coaches" whose entire job is to make your resume look better than it really is? Good question.

If you want to become an Executive in Sweatpants, the first step is archive your paper resume and begin building your "digital resume". Let's take a look at how to get started.

Chapter 6:
The New "Digital You"

So you're ready to start a new chapter in your career by building your digital profile. Now what? The great thing about oDesk and other platforms is that getting started is super easy (and free!). Setting up a profile is much like setting up an account on Facebook or other social media sites.

In order not to bore you, I'm going to focus on the strategy behind each step of the account setup process. If you are looking for an extremely detailed, step-by-step tutorial for setting up an account, refer oDesk's extensive FAQ section on their website.

A Few Comments Before You Get Started

Remember, it is crucial that you invest the time upfront to make your profile attractive to prospective clients. As I mentioned, your oDesk profile is much like a LinkedIn or Facebook profile, except you use it to make money! The basic idea is quite similar to most social media accounts. You create an account, add your background information, build out your profile, upload a photo of yourself, and you're ready to go. The difference between oDesk and social sites is that you are not looking to build virtual "connections" with other oDesk users per se. Rather, you're looking to connect through business service contracts.

Users of oDesk essentially fall into one of two categories: "contractors" and "clients". So if you're looking for work, you need to build your profile so that you stand out against other contractors. There are thousands of other contractors on oDesk. The good news is that you can build out your profile to accentuate your area of expertise. oDesk allows you to pick from hundreds of categories and subcategories that match your professional experience (see later sections of the book for examples). My theory is that you can't be all things to all people; therefore, take a considerable amount of time to think about your area of expertise and build your profile around this.

For Beginners: The Basics of Your Contractor Profile

Once you have created your oDesk account and gone through the basic setup steps, you will be able to get into the "meat" of your profile. oDesk is set up in a very intuitive way. All jobs that are posted are categorized based on the skill set that is being sought. Let's take a look at how I've set up my personal profile on oDesk. As I mentioned, my background is in marketing and business strategy. These are obviously broad categories of expertise. oDesk has already thought about that and broken such skill sets down into common **"categories"**. Within my profile, I simply select the categories that best describe my specific interests. In doing so, oDesk will know not to recommend me to prospective clients looking for a Certified Public Accountant or someone specializing in law. Rather, it will include me in searches pertaining to marketing. On the next page is a screenshot of what I've selected as my preferred categories in oDesk.

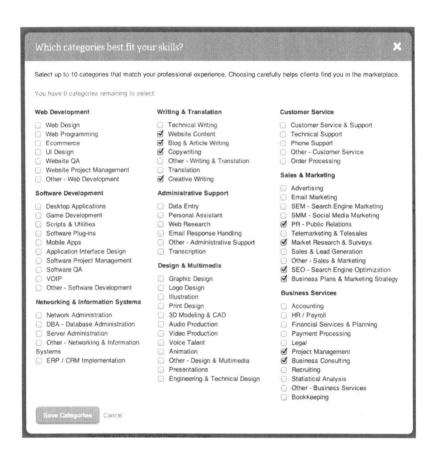

In addition to identifying your categories of interest for employment, oDesk also gives you the ability to drill down into even more specific skills. Within the **"Skills"** section of your profile, you click "Add" and start typing some of the things you're good at. In the screenshot on the next page, I simply typed in the word "marketing" and countless results appeared in the drop down menu. In this section of your profile, I suggest you be very mindful about the skills you select. You don't want to limit yourself to a skill that is "too specific", especially if you're trying to position yourself as a manager. Yet, at the same time, you don't want to select skills that are unrelated and do not make sense together. Take a look at the 5 skills I have identified. My strategy has consistently been to position myself as a "top-level" marketing and business strategy executive. As such, I have selected skills that are somewhat general in nature. I know a lot about email marketing and social media; however, I haven't selected them as skills because they do not align with my positioning strategy on oDesk.

Once you've identified your preferred categories and skills, I strongly suggest you begin building out your **oDesk portfolio**. In my opinion, this might be one of the most underrated parts of a contractor's profile. Think of this section as a virtual file folder of your past work. If you're a web developer, you can post links or thumbnails of your past work for all to see. If you're a writer, you can add selections of content you have developed for other clients. If you're an accountant, perhaps you can get a client's permission to post some financial analyses. Whatever your trade, it is critical that you thoroughly build this section out. Companies like to minimize risk when making hiring decisions. Your profile is the perfect place to show potential clients that you are legit. I suggest posting at least 5 different projects into your portfolio. You should also make a commitment to yourself to keep this portfolio fresh with recent and relevant work.

One additional side note about your portfolio: I believe it is imperative that you upload an "image" for each project (see next screenshot). Most prospective clients aren't going to go through every project you list. Therefore, having nice descriptive images will make your portfolio appear more robust. When looking at the entirety of your portfolio, clients are more likely to gain a positive impression if you have some diversity in your listings. Logos are especially effective, as they typically have prominent subject matter in the foreground and communicate a level of professionalism.

Additional Parts of Your Profile

oDesk gives you several other features in your profile, such as a profile title, objective statement, education history, certifications, and experiences. You can also upload a photograph of yourself. I'm not going to spend a ton of time on discussing these sections, as they are pretty straightforward. However, I will point out that the section "above the fold" on your profile (i.e. the section toward the top of your profile) requires considerable thought and planning. A unique title and objective statement gives you an opportunity to convey a favorable message. Having looked at many oDesk profiles, I believe some contractors could improve their profile by picking a better photograph. I have to laugh when I see the expression on some contractors' faces. It is almost like they were surprised that someone was taking a picture of them - then they uploaded it to their profiles. Put on a professional shirt and get in front of a normal background. Also, remember to smile - look like you want to work for someone.

The End Product: Your New "Digital Look"

After you've invested the time to build out your profile, it's time to take a step back and look at the end product. I suggest you have a few of your friends or relatives take a look and provide you with feedback. Go back and make adjustments as needed to present yourself in an effective manner. On the next page is a screenshot of my current profile. You will notice that there is a section called "work history and feedback". Obviously, when you're first getting started, you will not have anything listed here. However, this screenshot gives you a general idea of what a professional oDesk profile looks like. Notice the photo, profile title, skills, and objective statement fit together nicely to convey my message. When a prospective client reviews my profile, he or she can quickly understand my expertise. I'm not trying to be all things to all people; rather, I have a narrowly focused approach.

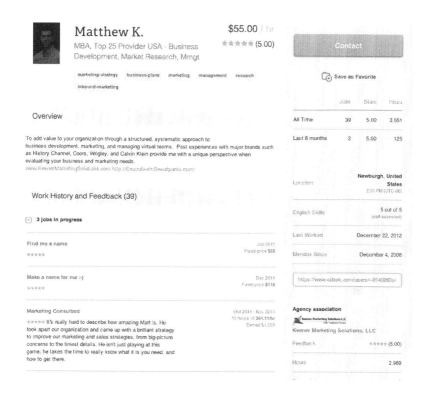

How To Pick A Starting Hourly Rate

In the previous screenshot, you might have noticed my hourly rate is $55 per hour. Let me assure you, that was not my initial rate on oDesk. If you recall from earlier in the book, I had just randomly stumbled upon oDesk after some of my other income ideas had fizzled out. At the time I figured anything is better than nothing, so I set my hourly rate at $10 per hour to see if I could get any nibbles. Doing the math in my head, I realized that 10 hours of "side work" per week would be an extra $400 of income per month. Looking back, I think this actually is a great strategy. Instead of demanding what I was actually "worth" at the time (which in 2008 was probably about $20 per hour), I swallowed my pride and took a chance. I suggest that you take a similar approach when getting started on oDesk. With a professionally built profile and an attractive hourly rate, you will be in a better position to get work quickly.

A word to the wise - oDesk and other marketplaces are not charities. They are in business to make money. When you're setting your hourly rate, you need to keep in mind that oDesk will take 10% of everything you earn. In my opinion this is a bargain. I bring this up now so that you factor this into your pricing strategy. For example, when I set my first hourly rate, my actual published rate (including oDesk fees) was $11.11. I understood that oDesk would be keeping $1.11 of every $11.11 that I earned. This netted me my desired $10 per hour. When bidding on new contracts, it is important you build oDesk fees into your proposal.

Chapter 7:
Let's Make a Deal

You've built your profile, and you're now ready to get some work. Although it is possible that someone might recruit you right off the bat, there are some additional steps you should take to properly prepare yourself. Sitting on your hands and waiting for something to happen is not a good strategy. In this chapter, we will take a look at some things you should do to get clients.

First Take Some Tests - Prove You're Worth Something

Another cool feature that oDesk offers its contractors is the ability to take free competency tests. In a "traditional" job, it is common for a human resources department to require applicants to take an assessment test. Employment on oDesk is not any different. In fact, the argument could be made that screening tests are even more important in a virtual environment. Before a prospective customer can hire you, oDesk requires you to take its "oDesk Readiness Test". This test is a very basic exam about how the time tracking system works, best practices, and other fundamentals. Once you have passed this test, it is very important to search for other tests in your field of expertise. By passing tests, you prove to the market that you are competent. In addition, oDesk rewards you by allowing you to apply for additional jobs based on the number of passed tests.

If you look closely at the screenshot on the next page, you will notice that there is a column that says "Status". oDesk gives you the option to make your test scores either public or private. By making a score public, you are giving prospective employers the ability to review your results. If you take a test and don't score well, oDesk allows you to

My Tests

Actions	ID	Taken on	Test	Score	% ▼	Rank	Duration mins	Success	Status
[make public] [embed]	299906	12/06/2008	U.S. English Basic Skills Test	4.50	93%	21919	29	Passed	Private
[make private] [embed] [Share on:]	1732509	09/28/2010	Business Strategy Test	4.25	90%	247	22	Passed	Public
[make private] [embed] [Share on:]	1732455	09/28/2010	Marketing Terminology Test	3.00	82%	908	16	Passed	Public
[make private] [embed] [Share on:]	297712	12/04/2008	oDesk Readiness Test for Independent Contractors and Company Managers	4.80			35	Passed	Public
[make public] [embed]	300127	12/06/2008	Telephone Etiquette Certification	4.00	62%	16722	10	Passed	Private
[make public] [embed]	300117	12/06/2008	Office Skills Test	3.90	71%	30724	31	Passed	Private

keep the score private and re-take it at some point in the future. This allows you to avoid the embarrassment of a potential customer seeing results you don't wish to publish. You will notice that I have chosen to make private three tests: Microsoft Word 2003 Test, Office Skills Test, and Telephone Etiquette Certification. (According to the test results it appears I didn't take the "Telephone Etiquette Certification" test very seriously - yikes!) I've chosen to hide these tests for two reasons. First, the most obvious reason is due to the score I received. Perhaps a more important reason is the relevancy of each test. Keep in mind that I'm selling myself as a high-end marketing consultant. Most of my clients could care less if I'm a wizard at Microsoft Office or Office Skills.

My main point here is to stress the importance of taking relevant oDesk tests, getting good scores, and then promoting these results on your profile. Building an attractive test record will help you stand out in the crowd and make you feel more confident when selling yourself to prospective customers.

Be Comfortable Selling Yourself

For some people reading this book, the section I'm about to discuss might be the "show stopper". I've noticed that there is a large segment of the population (even among professionals) that is completely resistant to doing any type of "sales" activity. Why is this? I think that there are several factors that contribute to this mantra. It may have to do with differences in personality type. Obviously God made us all different. Each person has his own strengths and weaknesses. Some people are just more comfortable than others in a sales situation.

But if you think about it, we are all constantly selling something. For example, we husbands are always trying to sell our wives on getting to play more golf. Wives often sell their husbands on going shopping. We try to sell our children on eating their vegetables and brushing their teeth. In fact, I would wager that you've made several "sales pitches" today already. If we're such good salesmen to those we know and love, why is it so uncomfortable to sell to people with whom we are less acquainted?

The difference is that most of us spend our lives trying to avoid uncomfortable situations. Stepping outside of our comfort zone instantly makes us feel less certain. Many people stay within their comfort zone until it no longer exists, prompting them to find their next comfort zone. This cycle continues over and over, yielding a life of significant emotional peaks and valleys.

While it is human nature to find a comfort zone, we must recognize that comfort zones are either expanding or contracting. I would argue that when your comfort zone is expanding, it is an indication that you are becoming lazy and/or complacent. Getting too comfortable opens yourself up to others moving in and making your services less valuable or even obsolete. This leads to a rapid contraction of your comfort zone. With a rapid contraction, you are forced to make quick decisions to get back to a more comfortable place. Successful people force themselves to contract their own comfort zones. By being open to making sales calls, learning new things, and working long hours, you make yourself "less comfortable" by choice. However, in doing so, you can almost guarantee yourself a truly consistent comfort zone with fewer emergencies to deal with.

In my experience, selling yourself is not nearly as hard as selling a physical product. I firmly believe that human capital is still something companies are willing to invest in. I began to realize this when working for the start up company I mentioned earlier in the book. At one point, I was working for at least a month to convince a major brand to spend $5,000 on 3D promotional items. They priced us against five other competing solutions, and eventually we lost the deal (because we were $.10 too high per unit). At the same time, I was negotiating a consulting deal on oDesk for $25 per hour (keep in mind that my starting hourly rate on oDesk was only $10 per hour, so this was a big deal for me!). All in all, I spent about 50 hours trying to get the $5,000 deal that would have only yielded $500 in gross income for the company (which would have been immediately consumed by overhead costs). On the other hand, my oDesk contract took me about 30 minutes to procure and yielded pure profit to my personal bottom line.

So what's the moral of this story? Companies understand there is still a market value for skilled labor. Tangible products can easily be commoditized, regardless the level of specification. Therefore, if you can provide a compelling service at a fair price, you will attract customers. The company has already made the decision to allocate its budget to such services...why would anyone else be a better fit than you?

Interview Checklist

So you've been invited to your first interview from a prospective oDesk client - now what? In preparation of your first interview, I've put together the following checklist. To this day, I still follow this process when preparing for an interview with a prospective client.

The Basics - The web has changed everything. You need to make sure that you are familiar with some common ways your interview may occur.

- **By Phone -** I typically offer to call the client at a time that fits his or her schedule. I also provide my direct line in case he or she wants to call me.

- **By Skype -** Skype is a free voice-over-ip system that allows you to have video calls with other people. I would say that about 50% of all of the business calls I make are via Skype. In order to use Skype, you have to create a free account and install the software on your computer. Make sure your Internet connection is fast enough to handle video calls. You will also want to get a decent webcam.

- **By Web Conferencing Service -** The most common web conferencing service is Gotomeeting. However, there are many free alternatives. Some require you to install software, while others do not. Just make sure that you have a little time in advance of the call to install the necessary software and review the dial in information. Also, make sure your Internet speed can handle this type of conference.

Research - Don't just go into the interview cold turkey. You must do some homework in advance and be prepared to intelligently discuss the prospective client's needs. This is the process I typically follow to learn more about the company:

- **Website Research -** If the prospective client has not given you much information about the company, it is suitable to request more info in advance of the call. You can easily send an email from your oDesk profile to request the company's website and any marketing literature they may have. Many times, the prospect will send you this information without having to request it. Once you have the company's URL, go through the site and try to understand their basic business model. I usually ask myself the following questions when reviewing a prospect's business model:

 – What industry and market(s) does this organization serve?
 – Do they appear to have a proven business model and revenue stream?
 – What appears to be this company's strengths and weaknesses?
 – Does this company provide me any "inside information" from their website? (things to consider: sales history, number of employees, major accomplishments)

• **Social Media Research -** A quick Google search for the contact's name usually returns several social media profiles (LinkedIn, Jigsaw, Facebook, and other sites). You can often gather interesting information that may help you prepare for the interview.

• **oDesk Research -** Does this prospective client have a good / bad feedback history on oDesk? A "good" feedback history would be 4 out of 5 stars (or greater). A "bad" feedback history would be anything less than 3 out of 5 stars. No feedback is sometimes scarier than bad feedback!

• **Competitor Research -** It can be quite effective to learn about your prospective client's competitors, especially if you are interviewing for a sales or marketing position. In my case, it often comes up in the interview that the company is looking to become "more competitive" in its marketing efforts. Having a basic understanding of the competitive landscape can help establish your commitment to the prospective client's needs.

Once you've done this preparation, you're all set to have the interview with your prospective client.

Get Started - Don't Be Too Picky

The interview went very well....now what? I typically like to send a thank you email after the meeting and remind the person that I am very interested in the opportunity. In your follow up email, it is important to include a "call to action" that politely requests the prospect initiate the contract on oDesk. The email can be very short and follow this template:

> *Dear Mr. Smith,*
>
> *Thanks again for speaking with me today about the opportunity with your organization. I really feel that there is a good fit between your company's needs and my skillset. I am excited to get started on the project.*
>
> *If you are ready to get started, please send over the offer this afternoon via oDesk. I will kick off the project upon accepting your offer.*
>
> *Thanks again,*

In my experience, most clients are as ready to get started as you are. By reminding them to send you the offer, it shows that you are serious about the contract. This also serves as a "to-do" for the prospective client, many of whom are innately task-oriented people. I prefer to give a suggested timeline (i.e. "this afternoon") to move the client to action before the excitement wanes.

Some may argue that you shouldn't take the first contract offer you receive. I have to admit, I am pretty selective about the clients / assignments I take on. However, this did not happen overnight. It ultimately comes down to supply and demand. If you are in high demand, you can be more selective. If you are in low demand (i.e. you don't have any contracts), I would argue that you should be less selective. You always want to be doing business with reputable organizations and people, but in general I suggest you take the contract and get started on oDesk. Your ultimate goal should be to make some money, provide an outstanding service, and drive for 5 star feedback from your client.

Caution: Fixed Price Versus Hourly

Here's an important note about contracts on oDesk (and probably other similar freelance sites, for that matter): clients can award two different types of contracts. An "hourly" contract is the most similar to typical employment. The company hires you on an ongoing basis to perform a given task. A "fixed price" contract is exactly what it sounds like - the company hires you to provide a certain deliverable or outcome in exchange for some agreed to dollar amount. I've taken on both types of contracts, but I typically prefer long-term hourly agreements. Fixed price jobs are good for when I'm asked to develop something tangible, such as a business plan or marketing analysis.

Using oDesk to Bill Time

As I've mentioned in previous sections, oDesk is especially unique because it provides several services for both contractors and clients. One important feature is oDesk's time tracking software. I won't go into the technical details of how it works, but ultimately here is an overview:

- You install the software on your computer.

- When working on a client's contract, you run the software and bill hours to that client account.

- oDesk automatically keeps track of how much time you billed to that client and simultaneously takes screenshots of your computer to ensure you're not goofing off.

- Based on the time you billed in a given week, money is transferred from your client's account into your account.

One Client Is Just the Beginning

Up to this point, we have focused on getting your first client. Now that I've provided you with a game plan to do so, the next section of the book will cover how to leverage this business model into a long-term career.

PART III:
SUSTAINING SUCCESS

Chapter 8:
Building Your Client Base

Getting your first client is a great accomplishment, but it's difficult to make a career out of a single client. In my experience, most oDesk clients are not interested in hiring contractors to a full-time gig. Most of my long-term contracts range between 5 and 20 billable hours per week. You should look at this as a great opportunity. Instead of having to put all of your eggs in the basket of a single employer, you can diversify your own risk by having many clients. This chapter will examine some of the most important things you can do to build your customer base and achieve long-term success.

The Importance of 5 Star Feedback

Sometimes I wonder if I'm a little bit obsessive compulsive. I always check several times to make sure the doors are locked before going to bed. Before meetings I always triple check my notes to make sure I know the material backwards and forwards. When it comes to my feedback score on oDesk, I'm especially sensitive. Regardless of how great I make myself sound, ultimately the proof is in the pudding (or in this case, the proof is in your feedback score). As I mentioned, the oDesk community is based on a feedback system similar to that of Amazon or eBay. If you do a great job, typically you are rewarded by the client with an appropriate feedback score. Over time, you build up many feedbacks that reflect the type of contractor you truly are. This overall feedback score impacts how your profile shows up in the search results and filters on oDesk, which are used by prospective customers.

To manage your oDesk reputation, I strongly suggest that you take several steps. First, during the course of your project you should periodically ask the client if you are meeting expectations. This simple step shows the client you are dedicated and also illustrates your desire to get their feedback. Once the project draws to a close and you have provided the final deliverable (if any), I always ask the client to leave me a 5 star review on oDesk. Typically the email goes something like this:

> *Dear Mr. Smith,*
>
> *Thanks again for your business. I really enjoyed working with you on this project. Please feel free to close the project and leave me a 5 star review on oDesk. I will reciprocate with a 5 star review for you, as you've been a pleasure to work with.*
>
> *Thanks again,*

Notice how I specifically asked for a 5 star review. If you did a great job, you should be rewarded appropriately. It is never inappropriate to ask for the best review possible if you indeed deserve it. In addition to the number of stars, clients can also leave a written summary of how you performed on the contract. Here are some of the more favorable reviews I've received from happy clients:

> *It's really hard to describe how amazing Matt is. He took apart our organization and came up with a brilliant strategy to improve our marketing and sales strategies, from big-picture concerns to the tiniest details. He isn't just playing at this game: he takes the time to really know what it is you need, and how to get there.*
>
> *Matt is a fantastic asset for our company. He uses creativity and deep knowledge of marketing to build up a "tidal wave" of incoming leads. With his help, our SEO ranking has gone from somewhere on page 10 to the #1 slot for some of our most important keywords, and we've seen the number of well-qualified leads jump significantly*

as a result. Matt consistently works to very high quality standards, which is important as we try to build a long-term brand. On top of all this, he is quite adept at managing teams and currently oversees our entire marketing effort. I feel very comfortable recommending him to the highest degree.

Insist On Regular Meetings with the Client

Looking back at some of my most successful client endeavors, one common thread seems to be good communication. If you think about it, a "normal" job is much more conducive to facilitating communication than remote work. If a manager needs to speak to one of his teammates, he can easily walk over to the employee's desk and discuss the topic face-to-face. In a remote setting, it becomes a bit more challenging. The natural tendency is to let communication fade over time, thus creating a divide between the goals of the manager and the worker. Therefore, I feel it is crucial that you proactively schedule recurring meetings with your clients. These meetings can be held over the phone; however, I prefer to get as much face time as possible via Skype.

Another side benefit of hosting regular client meetings is that it sets some boundaries on their expectation of your time. Some clients, if left to their own devices, can abuse your time by calling you every day to discuss every detail. By setting up recurring meetings, clients feel comfortable knowing that they can save up their ideas and discuss them all at once. This keeps your clients happy, while helping you remain efficient and sane.

Gathering New Clients While Maintaining the Core

Once you've settled in with a few "regular" clients, it is important to push yourself and identify additional prospective clients. Just like any job, it is a good idea to fill at least 40 billable hours per week. Some combination of hourly and fixed price projects can make this a reality. Earlier in my career on oDesk, I was more apt to take fixed price projects. It seems to me that fixed price jobs are somewhat easier to win than hourly ones. This is great for new contractors looking for experience and feedback.

I will pause here to point out one important caution. When you're browsing fixed price contracts, you will notice there are many $50 projects (or less) that seem quite easy at first glance. In my experience, these types of projects are potential landmines for your feedback score. One of the few "easy" $50 projects I took on involved re-wording the verbiage in a sales letter. The client provided me a pre-written letter and just asked me to critique it and provide any necessary edits. I did this within an hour of work and felt good about my theoretical $50 hourly rate. Needless to say, I was surprised when I got an email from the client telling me they actually wanted me to totally re-write it. After about 5 different versions, my actual hourly rate on this project was only a few bucks. To top things off, the client left me a feedback slightly less than 5 stars. I was able to convince them to update the feedback score to 5 stars; however, it really steamed me. From that point forward, I became a little bit more skeptical about projects that seemed too good to be true.

As you fill up your week with client work, it will become more difficult to keep everything balanced. Unlike a "normal" job where you're focusing on the interests of a single company, as an Executive in Sweatpants you must provide excellent service for all of your clients. Adding new clients is no excuse for falling behind with other clients. I use several tools to keep everything organized. Each week, I use a simple hour tracking spreadsheet to list out how many hours I will be working for each client and on which day(s). As each hour passes during the day, I update the "actual" hours worked next to the "planned" hours column. Not only does this provide me with a game plan, it also helps me track things like capacity and expected cash flow. I'll discuss this spreadsheet in more detail in the next chapter. In addition, I use a simple notebook to write out specific tasks that need to get done. This complements the usage of a project management system such as Basecamp or FreedCamp (many of my clients assign me tasks via their Basecamp account).

Your Two Greatest Assets

In my years of working as an oDesk contractor, there are two things that separate the successful people from the failures: integrity and reliability. Having hired contractors myself, I can personally attest to this. You may find someone who appears to have the exact credentials you are looking for, yet after you hire them they disappear and stop returning your emails. Likewise, you may find out that the contractor is not as ethical or honest as you had hoped. Although this creates hiring issues, it also presents a huge opportunity for you as a contractor. This is especially true if you are looking to build long-term client relationships. If you are always reliable and ethical, you can almost be guaranteed good results.

Good Billing Relations

In many instances, clients that hire you to an ongoing contract are doing so because they have a certain level of trust with you. As I've mentioned, it is more complicated to find good people in a virtual work setting than in a normal business setting. Because of this trust, it is important that you are always honest and ethical in your billing practices. Most clients will give you a maximum number of billable hours per week. The understanding is that you will bill only the number of hours needed in a given week to achieve your goals. If your limit is 10 hours per week, you may only need 5 hours in certain weeks while during others you may need 9 or 10. I've known contractors who always max out their hours each week and then beg for additional hours via email. This creates friction with clients and could be a red flag that you are being unethical in your billing practices. I strongly suggest that you set clear expectations and always maintain excellent communication with the client. The last thing you want to do is have clients questioning your judgment or character.

Good Client Relations

An important part of becoming an Executive in Sweatpants is maintaining a long-term perspective. It is important you always give clients a clear indication that you are invested in their long-term success (and mean it, of course). Subtle things can make a big difference. When a client hires me, I instantly begin referring to "our" goals and things that "we" can do to be successful. Notice how I'm not referring to "their" goals or things that "they" can do. This may seem like a small detail, but I believe it should not be overlooked. You want to be part of their team and always show that their goals are your goals. Another thing I like to do is send my clients Christmas cards with a small gift (usually a gift card to a restaurant chain or Starbucks). Customers really appreciate this type of thing, and it shows you are willing to go above and beyond to take care of them.

Increasing Your Published Hourly Rate

In the long run, the best way to ensure your financial stability is to increase your hourly rate. I would argue that you should follow a systematic process for doing this. Your goal should be to gradually increase your published hourly rate and approach the market rate for your services. If you're a lawyer, obviously the market rate tends to be much higher than an administrative assistant. Regardless of the services you provide, you need to be aware of the "going rate" for someone in your industry. My strategy has not necessarily been to renegotiate deals with existing clients; rather, I prefer to charge higher rates to new clients. As I mentioned earlier in the book, my initial hourly rate on oDesk was a mere $10. Currently, my newest clients are paying $55 per hour. I have every intention of growing this rate closer to $100 per hour. It has taken time and a lot of 5 star reviews to get where I am at now. If you provide excellent service and build trust with your clients, you too can grow your hourly rate and achieve success.

Why Limit Yourself @ 40 Hours?

There is one last point I want to make in this chapter. One of the beautiful things about not working for a big corporation is that you can dictate if you work "overtime". Most professionals who work for a large company end up working more than 40 hours anyway, but are not compensated for the extra time. As an Executive in Sweatpants, you get to determine what your "normal" workweek looks like. I've settled in at about 50 billable hours per week, which seems to be a good fit for me. Keep in mind that you will probably have at least 3 to 5 hours of additional administrative work each week (for accounting, continuing education, sales prospecting, etc.).

Chapter 9:
Tracking Your Success

How do you know if you're successful if you're not tracking goals? Do you even have any goals? In my experience, you must set both big and small goals to be an effective Executive in Sweatpants. Although the dress code is casual, goal setting and tracking must be somewhat formalized.

What's Your <u>Big Motivator</u>?

I'm not going to lie - when you work from home there are certain things that can easily become distractors. I've often had the temptation to just take the day off and watch TV. But the problem with this is twofold. First, every hour that you're goofing off is an hour you could be earning money. Second, and perhaps most importantly, occasional laziness leads to regular laziness, which leads to failure.

If you've ever read anything by Jim Collins[5], you know about "big hairy audacious goals". I won't go into detail, but essentially, Mr. Collins has discovered that companies that set extremely "audacious" goals are often the most successful. These aren't boilerplate goals such as beating last year's sales revenue by 12%; rather, these are goals that are almost ridiculous to even consider.

As an Executive in Sweatpants, my "big hairy audacious goals" are mostly personal goals. Since my company consists only of one employee (me), it makes sense to be driven by big personal goals (especially early on in your organization's history). One of my biggest motivators has been paying off my house within a 5-year window. As ridiculous as this may seem to many people in today's culture, that is a huge motivator

---

5 JimCollins.com - http://www.jimcollins.com/article_topics/articles/building-companies.html

for me. I'm pleased to report that I believe this goal is attainable but certainly is a stretch.

So what's your big goal? What is something that is possible, yet not likely? How can you make it happen? What are some additional personal goals that you can set for yourself? What deadlines can you set to achieve these goals?

To get your creative juices flowing, I'll give you a sneak preview into some of my current goals:

- Pay off the house within 5 years

- Finish writing this book within 1 year of conceptualization (if you're reading this book, it means I met this goal!)

- Take my wife back to Jamaica within the next 18 months

- Commit to learning at least 1 new thing every work day

Visualize Your Goals Regularly - But Don't Overdo It

Once you have identified a few goals, it is important to write them down and look at them somewhat often. It can become easy to get mired down in the daily grind and lose track of your big picture goals. By taking a few minutes and visualizing yourself accomplishing the stated goals, you can keep yourself motivated and happy. I've even gone one step further. Each goal has a photo next to it, which helps the goal resonate in my brain. For example, the goal pertaining to my house has a photo of my home. Beneath the photo it says "Pay off the house within 5 years". I find this to be effective for the visualization process.

One important point about setting goals: don't overdo it. I've met people who just sit around for hours pondering what they "could" do. At a certain point, goal setting becomes counterproductive, and you should just get down to business. You can set the best goals in the history of the world, but if you never do the work they are worthless.

I like to compare goal setting to the lifestyle of a prairie dog. A prairie dog lives below the surface of the ground, occasionally popping its head out to see what's going on. You should spend most of your time working (i.e. "under ground") and then periodically take a step back (i.e. "pop your head out of the ground") to make sure your daily activities align with the bigger picture.

Setting Micro Goals

Once you have a firm vision of the "big picture" goals, it is vital that you set "micro goals" to keep yourself motivated. Your larger goals will never be accomplished if you don't implement a plan of action. I use a combination of the following goal types every single day:

Annual Goals: As the name implies, these are goals for the immediate year. I typically dedicate a full day in late December (near the Christmas holiday), where I can go "off site" and do a review of the previous year and a projection for the coming year. During this session, I take a look at the average number of hours I worked for each client, what succeeded, what failed, and what I can do next year to provide even more value. I then layout a "forecast" by determining expected revenues from each client. On the next page is a screenshot of my annual planning spreadsheet for each client (using fictitious numbers and client information, of course).

Note: *you can download the following spreadsheet (and all the others mentioned in this book) for free by visiting www.ExecutiveInSweatPants.com/free.*

Client #1		Client #2	
Avg. Hours / Week	RATE	Avg. Hours / Week	RATE
5	$20.00	10	$25.00
# of Minutes / Day for Client		# of Minutes / Day for Client	
50		100	
Weekly Earnings from Client		Weekly Earnings from Client	
$100.00		$250.00	

Client #3		Client #4	
Avg. Hours / Week	RATE	Avg. Hours / Week	RATE
15	$30.00	5	$20.00
# of Minutes / Day for Client		# of Minutes / Day for Client	
150		50	
Weekly Earnings from Client		Weekly Earnings from Client	
$450.00		$100.00	

Income Per Week	# of Weeks to be Worked	Est. Annual Income
$900.00	50	$45,000.00

Weekly Goals: Based on your defined annual goals, you need to have a weekly game plan that helps you track your progress. Below is the spreadsheet I use to plan and track each week's work. Notice that the left hand side of the spreadsheet lists the names of each client and the associated hourly rate (this is just sample data, of course). Each color represents a day of the week, starting with Monday and ending with Saturday. The bold font is the number of minutes I intend to work for that client in a given day. The non-bold font indicates the actual results. You will also notice that the bottom row shows forecasted earnings for the week, number of hours worked, and totals for each day.

	Net oDesk Rate	Enter Work Week # Here (52 weeks in a year)							
		Monday			Tuesday				
		Plan	Actual	$ Earned	Plan	Actual	$ Earned	Hours Planned	Hours Worked
Client 1	$ 17.50			0.0	30	30	8.8	0.5	0.5
Client 2	$ 20.00	120	120	40.0	160	160	53.3	4.66666667	4.66666667
Client 3	$ 31.50			0.0			0.0	0	0
Client 4	$ 45.00	200	200	150.0	240	240	180.0	7.33333333	7.33333333
Client 5	$ 40.00			0.0	90	90	60.0	1.5	1.5
Client 6	$ 32.50	60	60	32.5			0.0	1	1
Client 7	$ 20.00			0.0			0.0	0	0
Client 8	$ 22.50	90	90	33.8	80	80	30.0	2.83333333	2.83333333
Client 9	$ 15.00			0.0			0.0	0	0
Client 10								0	0
Admin Work								0	0
		470	470	256.3	600	600	332.1	17.8333333	17.8333333

Week's Earnings	Hours Worked	Avg Hourly Rate
$ 588.33	17.83333333	$ 32.99

Daily Goals: Based on your weekly goals, you should already have a good starting point for each day's work. Obviously, things change from day to day. If you are intentional with allocating your time, however, you can usually be successful in predicting the amount of time for each client. At the beginning of each day, I usually open my spreadsheet and figure out how many minutes I'm going to work for each client (again, refer to the bold font column for the given day). Based on this, I write out each hour of the day and decide which client will get that hour of my time. In addition, I like to write each client's name and list out a few goals. As the day progresses, I am able to cross off each hour/goal from my notebook. I update the spreadsheet throughout the day to keep a running tab of how much I've billed the client and how much time is left for the day/week. (In addition to using my notebook, I like to keep track of to-do lists by using web-based project management systems. Many of my clients use Basecamp, but I use a combination of FreedCamp and Google Docs for my own projects.)

Tracking Micro Goals & The Impacts on Big Goals

If you follow the plan I've outlined, you're already on the right track. At the end of each day or week, you will have measurable metrics to evaluate how you did versus plan. It truly is a great feeling to know you reached a goal.

In addition to tracking hours worked versus plan, it is critical that you track actual cash flow. The beautiful thing about oDesk is that you automatically get paid based on the hours worked. If you bill 40 hours in a given week, you automatically get paid for exactly 40 hours (no invoicing required). This makes cash flow tracking much easier, because you know exactly when payment is going to clear. In addition to using QuickBooks Online (the free version of course), I keep a separate spreadsheet that tracks each week's cash flow. This helps me gain a big picture view of weekly invoice totals and identify trends / issues that need to be addressed.

Calendar Week #	Gross Sales Receipts - This Week's Increase in Bank Account(s) During This Week	6 Week Rolling Average
1	$1,000.00	n/a
2	$1,050.00	n/a
3	$1,100.00	n/a
4	$1,150.00	n/a
5	$1,000.00	n/a
6	$1,025.00	$1,054.17
7	$1,075.00	$1,066.67
8	$1,100.00	$1,075.00
9	$1,150.00	$1,083.33
10	$1,000.00	$1,058.33
11	$1,050.00	$1,066.67
12	$1,100.00	$1,079.17
13	$1,150.00	$1,091.67
14	$1,000.00	$1,075.00
15	$1,025.00	$1,054.17
16	$1,075.00	$1,066.67
17	$1,100.00	$1,075.00
18	$1,150.00	$1,083.33
19	$1,200.00	$1,091.67
20	$1,250.00	$1,133.33
21	$1,200.00	$1,162.50
22	$1,225.00	$1,187.50
23	$1,250.00	$1,212.50

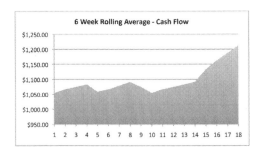

"Drifting" from oDesk

One final thought before we close this chapter. As you grow your business, it is likely that you will receive new referrals and make new contacts. Many of these new prospects may be unfamiliar with oDesk and want to hire you directly. This has happened to me lately. I've been hesitant to leave oDesk because it has been so good to me; however, at the end of the day it is my job to make customers happy. If they are uncomfortable using oDesk for some reason, I make it work. I still do work for some clients via oDesk, but not as much as I had in the past. It is good to stay active on oDesk to keep options open. I would not want to be in a situation where I was not billing any clients via oDesk. Some balance of oDesk and non-oDesk clients is probably a good mix once you've established your credibility.

Chapter 10:
Setting Boundaries

The idea of working from home is a relatively new phenomenon. With a traditional job you go to an office, put in your hours, and come home. Now technology such as smartphones has obviously blurred the lines between professional and personal time. However, at the end of the day, there is a rather clear line between your home life and work life because you physically leave the office. When you work from home, your office is your home. Your clients know that they can reach you any hour of the day since you are always "at the office". So how do you set boundaries to maintain a normal work / personal balance? Here are a few tips that seem to work well for me.

Set Reasonable Business Hours

During initial conversations with a new client, I am upfront about my "normal" business hours. I indicate that I am available every weekday from 7 am to 6 pm and Saturday from 7 am to 12 pm. I mention that I have several clients and do my best to balance time accordingly. There are times that I am unavailable (teleconferences, etc.), but I usually return phone calls within a few hours of a client leaving a voicemail. I also indicate that I do have a smartphone and read emails after work hours depending on my personal schedule.

Outside of normal business hours, I only look at my phone every hour or so. This way if there is an emergency I can be informed of it without driving myself totally crazy. In the 21st Century economy, I would argue it is almost impossible to be completely unplugged outside of normal business hours. Things change so rapidly that you need to check email occasionally when you're not "working". This is just something that comes with the territory of being an Executive in Sweatpants.

Be Prepared to Occasionally Say "No"

You may find that some clients fail to understand or respect the boundaries that you set. When you have clients in different time zones and with different business models, you will occasionally run into friction. I have had clients call me at 8:30 pm my time (when it would be difficult for me to bill them using oDesk). Is it unethical for me to not answer the phone? Is it unethical for the client to call me so late at night? I think these are all valid questions and depend on your relationship with the client. Typically, I try to be responsive to the client (as long as I'm not asleep). During family time I try to avoid long conversations and recommend we find a solution on the following business day if possible. Sometimes, however, this may not be possible, and I'll fire up the computer to help resolve the issue.

A client will occasionally push you to take on an additional role outside of your expertise. As much as I'd like to think I'm an expert on all things, I'm not. For example, one client wanted me to get involved with writing up contracts. After thinking about it, I pushed back and told the client I'd be glad to help think through the deal's structure, but they would need to find a lawyer to draft the agreements. Taking on too many things can cause you to become fragmented, inefficient, and exposed. Stick with what you know and become really good at it - there are plenty of customers who would love to tap into your expertise.

The "Honey-Do" List

Like most guys, my wife likes to add things to my "honey-do" list. My list usually includes lawn care, heavy lifting, technological issues (like backing up computers), bill paying, and general home maintenance duties. Considering that I'm at home all day long, it would be tempting to get a head start on my list. I'll admit there are occasions when I take a break to pay bills or take care of some urgent issue. But generally speaking, it is understood that between 7 am to 6 pm I'm focused on accomplishing work goals. My wife is awesome (I'm not just bragging, she really is!) and allows me to stay focused on work during those hours. We both understand that if I did not have the privilege to work from home, I would be working in an office somewhere. In other words, I recommend you over-communicate with your spouse to ensure you both understand work hour boundaries. The "honey-do" list can wait for the evenings and weekends.

Babies Crying in the Background

This may sound silly, but it is difficult to have a serious business conversation when your baby is crying in the background. Since my wife works outside the home, members of our family watch our son during the day. Occasionally, one of our relatives will come over and watch him at our home (instead of taking him to their own home). Keep in mind that our house isn't huge, so closing the door does not provide much of a sound barrier. On days like these, I try to avoid scheduling many meetings. The first word in the title "Executive in Sweatpants" is the word "Executive"; therefore, it is vital that I always portray a high level of professionalism. Having my son making noise in the background could jeopardize this reputation.

Other Distractions

Personally, I like to have the radio on while I work. I usually go with talk radio in the morning and music in the afternoon. However, you may find the radio to be more of a distraction than a benefit. That's fine - just know yourself and avoid things that make you unproductive. For example, I would not be able to work with a TV on. The combination of sound and video is enough to render me useless. As a result, I never have the TV on during work hours. The key is to know your optimal work environment and then put yourself in that type of situation.

Don't tempt yourself with distractions; otherwise, you will not get to keep your sweatpants very long.

Keep A Nice Shirt Handy

I remember a day early in my virtual career when a customer unexpectedly called me on Skype. I had just gotten out of the shower and was only wearing shorts (no shirt!). I knew that this client would want to see video of me while we talked. He also knew I was at my desk because I had just sent him an email. What did I do? After a second of freaking out, I sprinted to my closet, picked out a shirt, and got back in time to answer the call. After the call was over, I made a commitment to never put myself in that situation again. I typically wear a collared polo shirt in the summer time and a nice sweater in the winter. On the rare occasion that I'm wearing a t-shirt, I have a dress shirt close by in case I need it.

Get Some Fresh Air

As you take on new clients, it is tempting to just work straight through from early morning until evening. Although this is quite efficient, it is not an effective strategy. I've worked 10-hour days for several years now. At about hour number 8, my brain becomes overused. It is unfair for me to continue billing clients when I am not at the top of my game. To remedy this issue, I often go for a 20-minute jog. In doing so I can get some fresh air, blow off some steam, and stretch my legs. The exercise is good for health reasons too, of course. When I get back from my run, I take a quick shower and eat a snack. All together this only takes about 45 minutes. However, it always proves to be a wise investment of my time. I almost always get a second wind and typically come up with some good ideas while exercising. I highly recommend you implement a regular exercise routine to prevent burn out.

Unplugging on Sundays

My faith teaches me that I'm supposed to take it easy on Sunday and not do any work. I admit that I haven't always lived by this motto. In fact, I specifically remember a time when I worked for a month straight without taking a day off. In saying this, I realize that there are many professions that can't afford this luxury. Nurses, doctors, restaurateurs, firemen, farmers, and many other people have to keep the world going - even on Sunday. But as an Executive in Sweatpants, there really is no reason for you to work on Sunday. You have 144 hours Monday through Saturday to get your work done. If you can't get it done within the 144-hour window, it can probably wait until the next week. I don't just bring this up as a matter of faith; I bring this up because it is a basic human need to "unplug" one day per week. If you don't, you will find yourself feeling frazzled, fragmented, and frustrated.

I probably take this practice to an extreme, but I try not to even look at my email on Sunday. Now in the age of smartphones, it is almost impossible to go an entire day without checking email. I usually leave my phone in a place that makes it inconvenient to check it. This way, I only end up checking email a few times for the entire day as opposed to every 5 minutes (like I do during the work week).

If you can commit to unplugging on Sunday, you will find yourself more refreshed on Monday morning and much happier in the long run.

Chapter 11
You Must Keep Learning

You must avoid becoming so busy that you stop learning new things. When you provide a service, the client must be getting more value than what they pay you. The days of getting a college degree and never learning another thing are definitely over. So how will you stay on top of trends in your industry? Luckily, we live in a time with access to more information than ever. Below are a few steps I recommend to ensure you stay on top of your game.

Evaluating Your Strengths & Weaknesses

At heart, I'm a marketer - I'm not really an expert on the intricacies of website coding. Unfortunately, as an Executive in Sweatpants, your clients may not always have the budget to make up for your shortcomings. As such, it is your duty to fill the gap by educating yourself. The first step is to simply become aware of what you don't know. I'm somewhat embarrassed to admit that three years ago I had never heard the terms "robots.txt file" or "xml sitemap". However, I now use these tools daily to help my customers achieve their marketing goals. What concepts in your field of expertise are you are not aware of? Obviously, you may not know the answer to this question. In my experience there are two ways to answer this question. The first way is to have a client tell you about it. This can be quite embarrassing, considering that they are paying for your expertise. This has happened to me a few times; it's not my favorite way of learning about new things. The second way is to develop a continuing education system for yourself and stick to it. Here's how.

Developing a Continuing Education System for Yourself

Once you've identified your weaknesses, it's time to "formalize" your needs into a continuing education system. I use the word "formalize" loosely, as it doesn't need to be formal at all. It just needs to be something that you can commit to and benefit from. Think of the continuing education system like this: it should be a game plan for passively and proactively obtaining information. The goal is to make you a more valuable asset to your clients. There are many experts who have developed entire books around this process. In general, here is what I do to gather information:

Passive Processes - Below are a few tools you can use to receive information as it becomes available.

- **Industry Newsletters:** Sign up for email alerts / newsletters on topics pertaining to your trade. Smartbriefs is a free service that allows you to receive daily newsletters in your area of interest. I highly recommend using this free tool.

- **Google Alerts:** Google offers a lot of really cool tools that small business owners should utilize. One tool that I use quite often is called "Google Alerts". If you have a Gmail account, you can tell Google to automatically send you emails when certain topics get published on the web. This is an amazing productivity booster, and best of all it is free.

- **Social Network Groups & Alerts:** LinkedIn and Facebook both allow you to join various types of groups, based on your interests. There is a group for virtually every professional field. For my field of marketing, there are at least five LinkedIn groups that I've joined and get value from. In these groups, industry professionals discuss relevant current events and topics. Even if you choose to never participate in the conversation, you can sign up to receive periodic email alerts on popular conversations. This is a great way to find out what other professionals in your field are talking about.

Proactive Processes - Below are some strategies I've implemented to be proactive in my pursuit of knowledge.

- **Daily Twitter / Flipboard Review:** When I was in college, I remember listening to an executive who said he would read at least five newspapers each morning. Today, you don't need a bunch of newspapers delivered to your house. Instead, you can use free apps to summarize the news into a single portal. Recently, I've been using a free app called "Flipboard", which melds news feeds into a magazine-like presentation. It makes learning something new much more enjoyable. Twitter is a really great tool too because you can follow companies and individuals that are experts in their fields. Check your Twitter feed every day, and you will be sure to learn something new.

- **Read Industry Blogs:** Most companies publish a blog. If you've never heard the term "blog" before, think of it as a webpage where companies can post brief articles that their customers (or the general population) might find interesting. For example, on my blog for www.ExecutiveInSweatpants.com, I publish articles about building a successful home-based consulting business. Since I'm a marketer, I like to follow blogs that are about web marketing. The beautiful thing about a blog is that the information is almost real-time in nature and provides a great platform to stay informed. Also, most blogs offer a free RSS (Really Simple Syndication) feed that you can connect to your Twitter or Flipboard app. This makes the learning process even easier and more enjoyable.

- **Download Free Whitepapers:** Before I became an Executive in Sweatpants, I had heard the term "whitepaper" before. But to be honest, it really did not mean much to me. However, I have learned that whitepapers are an excellent source of information. Companies often publish whitepapers to establish themselves as a "thought leader" on a certain topic. The theory is that by publishing valuable information into a free document, the company will build loyalty with the reader and eventually get their business. As a marketer, I love to publish whitepapers for this very reason. As an Executive in Sweatpants, I love to download whitepapers because I always learn something new. Also, whitepapers serve as a great resource if you ever need to go back and re-learn something.

- **Attend Webinars:** With the advent of tools like Gotomeeting and WebEx, many companies host "webinars". If you've never heard of a webinar before, think of it as a seminar you would attend at a conference center (minus the conference center). Many organizations maintain a calendar that lists their upcoming webinars. You can usually register for free and receive an email with all the details of the event. Then, on the day of the webinar, you simply click a weblink and begin listening to the presentation from the comfort of your home or office. Keep in mind that companies will often keep your information and invite you to future webinars. This is usually helpful, but sometimes they can send you too many invites and bog down your inbox.

Developing a Knowledge Archive

Have you ever stopped to think about how many new things you learn in a single day? If you're an Executive in Sweatpants, you have to learn a lot of things to stay competitive. Let's assume you learn three new things every day. If you work 300 days in a given year, this means you are learning almost 1,000 new things every year. I can't remember what I had for dinner yesterday, so the odds of me retaining all 1,000 things in my brain are very improbable. Therefore, you need to develop a "knowledge archive" to fall back on. Think of it as a living, breathing infrastructure of everything you've ever learned and may use again in the future. There are many free tools that can help you build a knowledge archive.

Gathering Third Party Resources

In the "olden days" people would gather brochures, pamphlets, newspaper clippings, magazine articles, and other dead trees in vertical file cabinets. The problem with this approach is pretty obvious: unless you're a master at organizing documents, you're probably going to end up forgetting where certain resources are stored. Today, there is no excuse for keeping physical documents in your knowledge archive. Below are a few tips that I recommend you consider as you build your archive:

- **Upload Documents to Google Docs:** If you're not already using Google Docs, you should definitely check it out. Think of Google Docs as a cloud-based document creation and storage tool. It's like Microsoft Office (Word, PowerPoint, etc.) combined with a storage infrastructure like Flickr. The beautiful thing about Google Docs is that you can upload virtually any type of file, and it converts it to Google Doc format. This allows you to edit and store the file in a virtual file cabinet. Google Docs provides a powerful function that allows you to search by keyword. In addition, each Google Doc is given a unique URL. This allows you to link to a file instead of always having to open and close Word documents (or other file types). Did I mention Google Docs is free?

- **Quick Idea Capture via Smartphone Apps:** We entrepreneurs always have a million ideas running through our heads. When we see a product or service that sparks our imagination, there needs to be a way to capture that thought before it dies. If I'm in a meeting with a client and an unfamiliar topic arises, I will typically write it down on a scratch pad of paper. Then, after the meeting, I'll go to my smartphone and launch an app that records me explaining the concept. This way, I can periodically go back through all the ideas and topics in the smartphone app and decide what to do with them. There are dozens of free smartphone apps that provide this basic, yet important function.

- **Leverage Social Bookmarking:** Here's my Twitter strategy: share things that I would want to reference at some point. I realize this strategy may seem basic, but I find that when I do this I am able to simultaneously help myself and build new followers. When I look back at my twitter feed (@KeenerMarket and @ExecInSweats by the way), I see a historical documentation of the things I learned about. It's a great way to kill several birds with a single stone.

- **Quick Reference Folder:** There are some items I occasionally need at a moment's notice. For example, I always forget how to perform bulk "find and replace" in Excel spreadsheets. I've found several really helpful articles that remind me how to do this. But when I'm working on a project, I don't want to have to dig through my Google Docs or Twitter feed. Instead, I keep a "quick reference" folder on the desktop of my computer. I've saved the articles as web archive files with titles such as "Excel - bulk find and replace" for quick reference. I can easily sort the list of references alphabetically, find the right article, and I'm on my way. Simple, yet effective.

Documenting Your Own Resources & Processes

Large companies often require employees to document procedures as a risk aversion measure or to qualify for certain quality standards. Having participated in such processes myself, it seems these practices rarely provide value to the company. Employees fail to take ownership of the process and create procedures within the boundaries of a rigid structure. As an Executive in Sweatpants, you have the flexibility to document your own secret procedures in the way that benefits you the most.

- **Create Screen Capture Videos:** If you're like me, reading a big long list of instructions is not the best way to remember how to do something. Instead, I like to create brief demo videos that explain certain procedures I've developed. The video can be created to display your computer's desktop with your voice providing narration. You can create quick, helpful videos that provide a refresher course on a given topic. There are several tools that allow you to do this, but I like to use Jing (for capturing the video file) in combination with Screencast (which is where the video is permanently stored for future reference). Screencast provides you a unique URL for each video and allows you to set certain privacy settings (public, private, etc.). This is especially important if you are documenting proprietary procedures that you don't want your competitors to discover.

- **Again, Use Google Docs:** Did I mention yet that I love Google Docs? With Google Docs you can create a unique document for each pertinent topic. This allows you to create links to related documents and easily build out a highly accessible information infrastructure. Stop digging through folders for an outdated Word document. Instead, edit your notes real-time from any web-enabled device. Did that sound like a commercial for Google Docs?

Hire People Who are Smarter than You

The problem with hiring people is that it costs you money (obviously). The upside is that you get to tap into their knowledge and leverage this information into more value for your customers. This translates into greater loyalty from your clients and more money for you. Hiring people is not always feasible though, especially when you're getting started, and cash is tight. But as you build your business, I recommend you begin to bring on contractors (via oDesk, of course) who can help you stay on top of your game.

One thing that I've been doing lately is hosting monthly meetings with contractors who are experts in marketing. Call it a "mastermind meeting" or whatever you like. The ultimate goal is for me to pick their brains and try to extract what I don't already know. I usually set a basic agenda for these meetings but leave it up to my contractors to fill in the gaps. Using AnyMeeting, we are able to have an interactive webinar that I can record and save for future reference.

Chapter 12:
Let's Go Shopping for Sweatpants!

Congratulations! If you follow the plan outlined in the previous 11 chapters, you will be well on your way to becoming an Executive in Sweatpants. Welcome to the club. Here are a few light-hearted considerations for building your work from home wardrobe.

Style Is Still Important

When I started working from home, I would just wear some old (we're talking high school baseball) sweatpants each day. Before long, I started to feel kind of lazy because of how I looked. I began to realize that my ratty old sweatpants were affecting how I visualized myself. It was not portraying the image that I wanted, regardless of the fact no one knew what I was wearing. (As an aside, back in high school I always heard teachers say that there were rarely fights at prom because people were dressed in tuxedos. I'm not sure if this is actually true, but the bigger point is that attire can impact behavior.)

To alleviate this issue, I decided to go shopping for some sweatpants that "looked like" dress pants. To my surprise, there are actually quite a few apparel companies that produce exactly what I was looking for.

Specific Things I Look For in Sweatpants

I'm pretty particular, so here are a few things that I specifically look for when picking out a pair of sweatpants for work use:

- **Material:** I prefer to go with pants made of a lightweight, almost mesh-like material that is comfortable and not too hot (I'm rather warm-natured).

- **Style:** For goodness sake, don't get the sweatpants with the elastic band at the bottom.

- **Color:** I like black or navy because I get the look of slacks with the feel of sweats.

What To Wear During Summer

You might be thinking, does he wear sweats all year round? No, of course not (but it wouldn't be a very catchy book title to say "Executive in Sweatpants...and Khaki Shorts!"). When it is warm, I prefer to wear dress shorts and a nice polo.

One Final Thought - Don't Let the Sweats Fool You

What you wear is probably irrelevant. The secret to becoming a successful Executive in Sweatpants is quite clear: work harder than you ever have before, continuously learn new things, fully exploit opportunities on oDesk and other sources, and don't take anything for granted. Best wishes in your pursuit of excellence...and sweatpants.

Bonus Chapter:
Secret Free Tools

I've mentioned several tools I use each day. Below is a listing of my favorite tools. I hope you find these to be helpful, as they are all great resources for my business.

1. **oDesk** - Visit http://www.odesk.com to get started with your free account.

2. **Google Docs** - Visit www.docs.google.com to sign up for a free Google Docs account.

3. **Google Voice** - Once you've signed up for Google Docs, you can use your Google ID to set up a Google Voice account. This gives you a unique phone number from which you can make outgoing calls from your computer, set up call forwarding, and receive transcribed email alerts when clients leave you voicemails. Learn more at https://www.google.com/voice.

4. **Google Apps** - Google offers business owners the ability to host multiple email accounts for a custom domain. Many of my clients rely on Google Apps' great services. Learn more at www.google.com/a.

5. **Skype** - Most people are familiar with Skype. It is the most widely used system for voice / video meetings between remote team members. Download Skype for free at: www.skype.com.

6. **FreedCamp** - This is a slick project management system that

allows you to manage multiple todo lists and collaborate with team members, clients, etc. Check it out at www.freedcamp.com.

7. **AnyMeeting** - It's like Gotomeeting, but for free. Learn more at www.anymeeting.com.

8. **MailChimp** - This is a great marketing tool that allows you to send attractive bulk emails. Sign up free at www.mailchimp.com.

9. **Pixlr** - Pixlr is a free, web-based photo editor (similar to Photoshop). It doesn't have as much functionality as Photoshop, but it gets the job done. Visit www.pixlr.com.

10. **Flipboard** - This is a really cool app that formats all of your favorite feeds, blogs, and content into a magazine-style experience. It makes learning new things more enjoyable. Download the app for free at: www.flipboard.com.

11. **Jing** - This is a free download for Mac or PC that allows you to capture screenshots and brief desktop videos. Get this tool at: www.techsmith.com/jing.html.

12. **Screencast** - Screencast is a free place to store and organize your Jing videos and screenshots. You can set certain privacy levels based on your preference. Sign up for a free account at: www.screencast.com.

13. **WeTransfer** - Need to send huge files? WeTransfer is a simple, yet powerful online service that allows you to quickly send giant files to people across the globe (or down the street). No account is required. Just visit www.wetransfer.com to send your first file.

Other tools I've developed...

- **Annual Planning Spreadsheet** - As I mentioned in Chapter 9, you should do some planning each year to identify your future income stream. This spreadsheet helps you quickly analyze what next year's revenue will look like, based on the hourly rate and workload assumptions. Download this spreadsheet for free at www.ExecutiveInSweatPants.com/free.

- **oDesk Hour Tracking Spreadsheet** - This might be the most important tool I've developed. When I think about all the documents I use on a daily basis, I refer to this document the most. This spreadsheet tracks the planned and actual hours worked per client per day. In addition, it calculates how many hours I need to reach certain weekly revenue goals. It helps me stay organized and ensures I bill clients the right amount of time. The spreadsheet takes into consideration the different hourly rates of all clients and shows total earnings for the week. Download this spreadsheet for free at www.ExecutiveInSweatPants.com/free.

- **Prospecting Efficiency Spreadsheet** - I might have gone a bit overboard on this spreadsheet. My ultimate goal was to track how efficient I am in getting new clients on oDesk. In the past, I've worked in industries that took countless hours just to close a small sale. I realized that on oDesk, I could quickly close new deals that wound up earning me tens of thousands of dollars in the long run. This spreadsheet is really more for my own enjoyment than anything else. Download this spreadsheet for free at www.ExecutiveInSweatPants.com/free.

- **Cash flow Spreadsheet** - This file will help you stay on top of your cash flow. Remember, if you do all your hourly billing on oDesk, payment for your work is guaranteed and happens automatically.

However, there are a few days of lag time between billing and payment. In addition, some clients may not be on oDesk. This spreadsheet helps assure cash flow projections are consistent with overall annual goals. Download this spreadsheet for free at www.ExecutiveInSweatPants.com/free.

Get All of These Tools Now - www.ExecutiveInSweatPants.com

Now that you've learned what it takes to become an Executive in Sweatpants, I want to arm you with the tools you need to succeed. Visit www.ExecutiveInSweatPants.com/free to get all of the free tools mentioned in this book (and many more). Check the site often for new free tools. You can also sign up to receive our blog feed via email. Best wishes!